When My Name Was Keoko

Linda Sue Park

TEACHER GUIDE

NOTE:

The trade book edition of the novel used to prepare this guide is found in the Novel Units catalog and on the Novel Units website. Using other editions may have varied page references.

Please note: We have assigned Interest Levels based on our knowledge of the themes and ideas of the books included in the Novel Units sets, however, please assess the appropriateness of this novel or trade book for the age level and maturity of your students prior to reading with them. You know your students best!

BN 978-1-58130-871-6

To order, contact your
local school supply store, or:

Toll-Free Fax: 877.716.7272
Phone: 888.650.4224
3901 Union Blvd., Suite 155
St. Louis, MO 63115

sales@novelunits.com

novelunits.com

Table of Contents

Skills and Strategies

Critical Thinking
Interpreting evidence, compare/contrast, forming opinions, identifying stereotypes, paradox, pros/cons, research

Comprehension
Cause/effect, classifying, details, generalizing, inferencing, main idea, predicting, summarizing

Listening/Speaking
Discussion, oral report, role-playing

Vocabulary
Compound words, context clues, synonyms, antonyms, using a dictionary

Writing
Article, description, list, narrative, letter, report, interview

Literary Elements
Analogy, characterization, description, foreshadowing, plot development, setting, point of view, simile, theme

Across the Curriculum
Art—drawing; Science—pine trees, cherry trees, rice, gliders; Social Studies—maps, culture, history, politics, laws; Math—statistics, percentages; Technology—Internet research

Genre: historical fiction

Setting: a town in southern Korea, 1940–1945

Point of View: first person, from two characters' points of view

Themes: national pride, family, cultural diversity, political disobedience, hardships of war, loss of freedom

Conflict: person vs. self, person vs. person, person vs. society

Style: narrative

Date of First Publication: 2002

Summary

The year is 1940. Ten-year-old Sun-hee and her 13-year-old brother, Tae-yul, live with their parents in Japanese-controlled Korea. The Japanese prohibit the expression of Korean culture, going so far as to require Koreans to adopt Japanese names. Sun-hee becomes Keoko, and Tae-yul becomes Nobuo. Their father, a vice-principal at a school, is secretly a writer for the Korean revolutionary movement, and their uncle, a printer, prints an underground Korean resistance paper. Sun-hee misunderstands a friend's warning and believes Uncle is in danger of being arrested by the Japanese. Uncle goes into hiding. As World War II heats up, Tae-yul drops out of school to work on a Japanese airstrip. The Japanese police question him about Uncle and want him to arrange a meeting, but Tae-yul dodges the task by saying he is reporting for duty as a soldier in the Japanese army. He eventually becomes a kamikaze pilot. His family believes he is dead after they receive a letter he wrote before his mission. Unbeknownst to the family, clouds obscure Tae-yul's target, and his flying group returns to base and is thrown in jail. At the end of the war, he is released, Americans occupy the southern part of Korea, and Uncle is trapped in the northern part of the country.

About the Author

Linda Sue Park was born and raised in Illinois. Her parents are Korean immigrants, and her stories come from her interest in her heritage. She earned degrees from Stanford University, Trinity College Dublin, and the University of London. Park worked as a copywriter and journalist before trying her hand at young adult novels. Park believes writers should first be voracious readers, which will make writing techniques an intrinsic part of the writing process.

Park's first novel, *Seesaw Girl*, was published in 1999 and earned excellent reviews. Her second book, *The Kite Fighters*, was also well received. *A Single Shard*, her third book, won the 2002 Newbery Medal. *When My Name was Keoko* also received many awards: ALA Notable Books for Children, ALA Best Books for Young Adults, Jane Addams Children's Book Honor Award, *Publishers Weekly* Best Books of the Year, *School Library Journal* Best Books of the Year, and IRA Notable Books for a Global Society.

Park and her husband live in Rochester, New York, with their two children and a dog. Her official Web site is www.lspark.com (active at the printing of this guide).

Major Characters

Sun-hee: ten-year-old Korean girl whose Japanese name is Keoko

Tae-yul: 13-year-old Korean boy whose Japanese name is Nobuo

Abuji: father of Sun-hee and Tae-yul; a school vice-principal

Omoni: mother of Sun-hee and Tae-yul

Uncle: Abuji's brother; a printer

Tomo: Sun-hee's Japanese schoolmate

Jung-shin: Sun-hee's Korean friend whose father is helping the Japanese

Mrs. Ahn: neighbor of Sun-hee's family

Initiating Activities

Choose one or more of the following activities to introduce the novel.

1. Multimedia: Show videotapes, pictures, and photographs of Korea and its people. Check out several books about Korea to use as resources throughout the study of the novel. Allow each student to look at a resource material for three minutes before passing it on to the next person. Continue passing resources around until students have seen most of the resources. Seeing pictures of Koreans and their country will give students background knowledge for the novel.

2. Maps: Show Korea on a world map and point out its proximity to Japan.

3. Science: Show a picture of rice fields in Korea and explain the unique way rice grows. Explain that rice is a staple in the Korean diet.

4. Culture: Show pictures of traditional Korean dress, homes, and planned gardens in the 1940s.

5. Math: Give statistics about population density and major cities in both North and South Korea.

6. History: Discuss the Korean Conflict, how Korea is now divided, and the role the United Nations plays in keeping the peace.

7. Social Studies: Discuss the family arrangement and the importance of honor and respect in Korean society. Contrast it with family arrangements in the United States.

8. Predicting: Give students the following clues and have them write a paragraph predicting what they think will happen in the story: World War II, Japanese occupation of Korea, kamikaze, traitor, underground resistance newspaper, Korean alphabet, Japanese names, and traditions.

Vocabulary Activities

1. Vocabulary Sort: Have students sort vocabulary words into categories (e.g., nouns, verbs, adjectives, and adverbs).

2. Sentences: Have students select three or four vocabulary words to use in one sentence. They may do this with the vocabulary lists for each section.

3. Word Maps: Have students complete word maps (see page 6 of this guide) for vocabulary words. For example: marathon (9), traditional (31), intricate (42), reign (59), supervised (86), endeavor (97), slander (117), legibly (123), procedures (133), and grudgingly (168).

4. Context Clues: Remind students of the various types of context clues such as description, example, synonym, contrast, and comparison. Examples of words from the novel to practice using context clue strategies include: wincing (13), anthem (19), mesh (44), realm (63), edible (95), revealed (146), and apology (183).

5. Vocabulary Charades: Have students act out some of the vocabulary words that relate to behavior and have other students guess which ones they are. Examples: embarrassment (9), disrespect (18), doubtful (40), reluctantly (112), and efficient (127).

6. Specific Categories: Have students list vocabulary words related to specific categories. Examples include: military terms—commandeering (75), allies (88), tactic (114), recruits (114), censored (122), casualties (154), bombardment (154), and maneuvers (156); sports—competitions (7) and marathon (9); and Japanese emperor—reign (59), divine (60), and realm (63).

7. Visual Images: Have students use an encyclopedia, the Internet, or other resources to find pictures of vocabulary words. Examples: assembly (19), trowel (33), mesh (44), brooch (75), authorities (82), and accommodations (109).

8. Word Map—Verb: Have students complete word maps (see page 6 of this guide) for the vocabulary verbs. For example: disobeyed (39), commandeering (75), contradict (85), inflicted (107), survived (141), and fidget (176).

9. Sentences: Have students choose words from the vocabulary lists and write a sentence about a main character and a sentence about themselves using the same words. For example: embarrassment (9), disrespect (18), doubtful (40), supervised (86), slander (117), extraordinary (140), and identity (174).

Word Maps

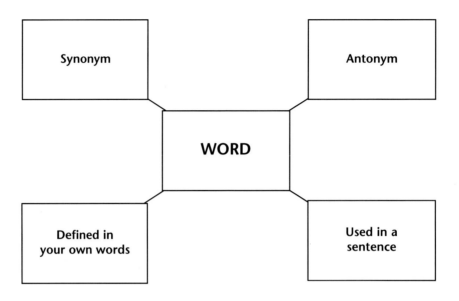

Word Map for a Verb

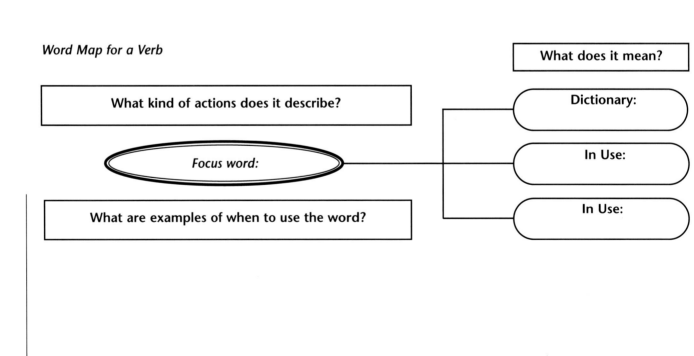

Using Character Attribute Webs

Character attribute webs are simply a visual representation of a character from the novel. They provide a systematic way for students to organize and recap the information they have about a particular character. Attribute webs may be used after reading the novel to recapitulate information about a particular character, or completed gradually as information unfolds. They may be completed individually or as a group project.

One type of character attribute web uses these divisions:

- How a character acts and feels. (How does the character act? How do you think the character feels? How would you feel if this happened to you?)

- How a character looks. (Close your eyes and picture the character. Describe him/her.)

- Where a character lives. (Where and when does the character live?)

- How others feel about the character. (How does another specific character feel about the character?)

In group discussion about the characters described in student attribute webs, the teacher can ask for backup proof from the novel. Inferential thinking can be included in the discussion.

Attribute Web

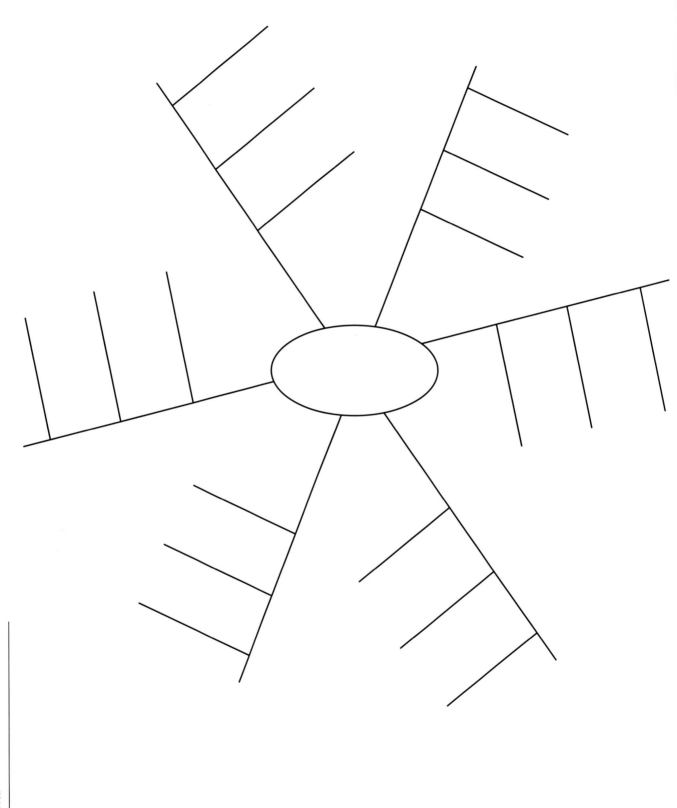

Story Map

Directions: Fill in each box below with information about the novel.

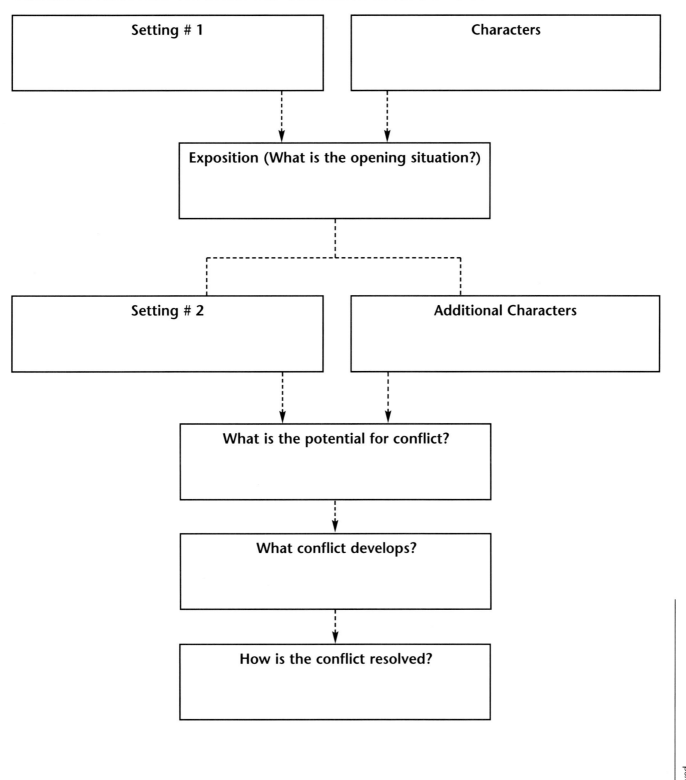

Setting # 1

Characters

Exposition (What is the opening situation?)

Setting # 2

Additional Characters

What is the potential for conflict?

What conflict develops?

How is the conflict resolved?

Metaphors and Similes

A **metaphor** is a comparison between two unlike objects. For example, "he was a human tree." A **simile** is a comparison between two unlike objects that uses the words *like* or *as*. For example, "the color of her eyes was like the cloudless sky."

Directions: Complete the chart below by listing metaphors and similes from the novel, as well as the page numbers on which they are found. Identify metaphors with an "M" and similes with an "S." Translate the comparisons in your own words, and then list the objects being compared.

Metaphors/Similes	Ideas/Objects Being Compared
1. Translation:	
2. Translation:	
3. Translation:	

Using Predictions

We all make predictions as we read—little guesses about what will happen next, how a conflict will be resolved, which details will be important to the plot, which details will help fill in our sense of a character. Students should be encouraged to predict, to make sensible guesses as they read the novel.

As students work on their predictions, these discussion questions can be used to guide them:
What are some of the ways to predict? What is the process of a sophisticated reader's thinking and predicting? What clues does an author give to help us make predictions? Why are some predictions more likely to be accurate than others?

Create a chart for recording predictions. This could either be an individual or class activity. As each subsequent chapter is discussed, students can review and correct their previous predictions about plot and characters as necessary.

Use the facts and ideas the author gives.

Use your own prior knowledge.

Apply any new information (i.e., from class discussion) that may cause you to change your mind.

Predictions
_____
_____
_____
_____

Prediction Chart

What characters have we met so far?	What is the conflict in the story?	What are your predictions?	Why did you make these predictions?

Inference Flow Chart

Directions: Fill in the boxes of the flow chart with the events portrayed in the story. In the ovals beneath, state what emotions and feelings are inferred.

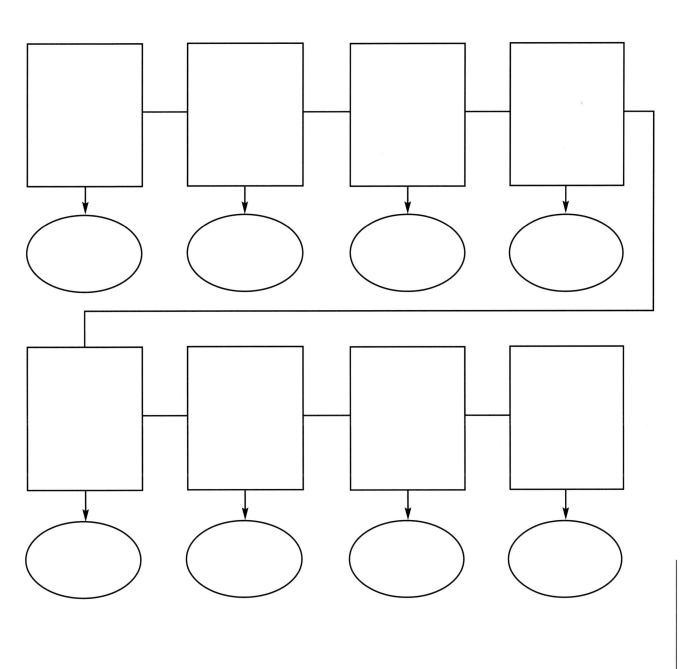

Chapters 1–4, pp. 1–15

In Japanese-occupied Korea in 1940, Sun-hee listens to her father and uncle discuss a rumor about a new law that is to be imposed on the Koreans by the Japanese Emperor. The Korean people, who must already speak Japanese in public, must now choose Japanese names. Tae-yul chooses the letter N from the dictionary and names himself Nobuo.

Sun-hee remembers four years earlier when her family was listening to the Olympics. A Korean runner won the marathon, but the announcer gave the runner a Japanese name and said he represented Japan. Later her uncle was beaten because he printed a newspaper article using the runner's Korean name and showing a Korean flag on his uniform. At home, Uncle drew the Korean flag for Sun-hee and Tae-yul, and then they burned the drawing. Uncle promised that someday they would raise the Korean flag again.

Vocabulary
competitions (7)
embarrassment (9)
marathon (9)
abruptly (9)
wincing (13)

Discussion Questions

1. Each chapter is titled by the name of the viewpoint character. Is this a good way for the author to show who is telling the story? Which do you like better—first-person or third-person stories? Why? Sun-hee's viewpoint is given in past tense. Tae-yul's is given in present tense. Which do you prefer? *(Because both viewpoints are in first person, it would be difficult to tell who was telling the story if the chapters weren't titled by the viewpoint character. Answers will vary on which style is liked better. First person portrays immediacy; Answers will vary.)*

2. Sun-hee thinks that "Ears don't close the way eyes do" (p. 1), and it's not her fault that she's listening to men's business, when she is actually trying to hear all she can. What does this say about her character? *(She's justifying her curiosity. p. 1)*

3. Abuji thinks of a way to secretly keep the meaning of the family name. What is this way? What does this say about the children's father? *(He shows them that the name means the same in both languages. He makes the best out of a bad situation, and he's a clever man. Answers will vary. pp. 5–6)*

4. What type of man is Uncle? What clues to his personality has the author given? *(He's funny, intense, proud of his heritage, and courageous. He makes up the Olympic commentator's words about the French carrying a long loaf of bread. He gets angry about a Korean running in the race under a Japanese name. He prints the Korean name of the runner and changes the picture to depict a Korean flag on his uniform even though he knows he will be punished for it. pp. 8–12)*

5. Tae-yul reassures Sun-hee that Uncle will be all right. What do Tae-yul's actions and his words in this situation say about his character? *(He is kind and caring and does not want her to worry. He holds her hand until she falls asleep. Answers will vary. p. 12)*

6. What do the black symbols on the Korean flag represent? Why does Uncle make the children memorize the look and meaning of the Korean flag and then burn the picture? *(Each represents a cycle: the seasons—summer, autumn, winter, spring; directions—south, west, north, east; the universe—sky, moon, earth, sun. It is illegal to have a representation of the Korean flag. p. 13)*

7. Why does Uncle say that someday Sun-hee will sew the flag and Tae-yul will raise it on buildings? *(He is optimistic that Korea will be liberated from Japan. pp. 14–15)*

8. **Prediction:** Will Sun-hee sew the Korean flag?

Supplementary Activities

1. Characterization: Begin Attribute Webs (see pages 7–8 of this guide) for Sun-hee and Tae-yul.

2. Plot Development: Begin a Story Map (see page 9 of this guide) to use as you read the novel.

3. Metaphors and Similes: Begin a list of metaphors and similes (see page 10 of this guide) and add to the list as you read. For example, "Uncle's face is red as a pepper" (p. 5).

4. Social Studies: Research pertinent information about Tan-gun, the founder of Korea.

5. Culture: Research Korean folktales and share them with the class through oral reports.

6. Research: What does your name mean? A name-the-baby book can be used as one resource. Interview your parents and find out who picked your name and why.

7. Art: Draw pictures of the Japanese flag and the Korean flag that Uncle describes. (It will be the current South Korean flag.)

Chapters 5–7, pp. 15–35

Abuji chooses the name Keoko as Sun-hee's Japanese name because it has the same meaning in both languages. She is punished at school when she forgets to use a student's Japanese name. Yet, she excels at learning kanji, the Japanese picture-character writing, and wins an award in school during her fourth year for her language skills. A gang of Korean boys calls her "lover of Japan" after she wins the award. She is ashamed, but her father tells her that the ancient writing comes from the Chinese and is used in both Japanese and Korean. Tae-yul does not excel in school. He is more interested in mechanical things. He and Uncle are building a bicycle together. The family eats millet, a chicken feed, because rice is scarce due to the war between Japan and China. A new law demands that the Korean national tree, the rose of Sharon, be dug up and replaced with the cherry tree, the national symbol of Japan. The children's mother has them plant the smallest rose of Sharon tree in a pot to keep in the workshop.

Vocabulary
disrespect (18)
assembly (19)
anthem (19)
traditional (31)
trowel (33)
trait (34)

Discussion Questions

1. Why does Sun-hee want to stay angry about losing her name? What does this say about her character? *(She sees the welts on her legs as a reminder of the whipping she received when she forgot a student's Japanese name. She doesn't want to forget that, despite the name change, she is still Korean. Answers will vary. pp. 16–17)*

2. Why is Sun-hee delighted that Tomo smiles at her with his eyes when she wins an award? *(Her Japanese friend is pleased for her even though he cannot acknowledge her presence because she is Korean and he is Japanese. p. 21)*

3. How does Abuji help Sun-hee with her kanji? *(He tells her the story behind the pictures. After she wins the award, he tells her that the Japanese writing was originally from the Chinese and is used in Korean writing as well. Learning kanji well honors her ancestors. pp. 20–23)*

4. Tae-yul knows his lessons, yet doesn't excel at academics. He feels it would be shameful if he didn't do adequately. Why? What does this say about his character? *(He doesn't want to dishonor his father, who is vice-principal. Answers will vary. p. 24)*

5. What does the Korean saying "Eat when you are eating, talk when you are finished" (p. 31) mean? Is this rude? *(It means give your meal due respect. Each culture is different, and what is considered good manners in one country, might be considered bad manners in another.)*

6. Why does Sun-hee believe the rose of Sharon tree planted in the pot will be the most beautiful tree in the world when it can be replanted outside? What does this say about her character? *(She knows that when the tree can be replanted, Japanese rule will have ended. She is very patriotic. Answers will vary. p. 35)*

7. **Prediction:** Will the rose of Sharon tree survive in the pot?

Supplementary Activities

1. Predictions: Begin a Prediction Chart (see pages 11–12 of this guide).

2. Metaphors and Similes: Add to your list of similes. Example: Sun-hee's calligraphy brush became "a creature light as a dragonfly, smooth as a snake, quick as a rabbit" (p. 20).

3. Writing: Practice calligraphy on a few letters and draw the kanji figures on pages 21, 25, and 26 of the novel.

4. Social Studies: Research the war between Japan and China that took place in Manchuria and discover why they were fighting.

5. Art: Draw pictures of a rose of Sharon tree and a cherry tree.

Chapters 8–11, pp. 35–59

Uncle's business is expanding, which means he is doing more work for the Japanese. Sun-hee and Tae-yul overhear a discussion between their father and uncle about danger. Uncle offers to leave, but Abuji tells him that this is his home. The children decide to investigate what Uncle is doing. Sun-hee takes a friend to Uncle's print shop after school. Uncle acts oddly when he hears that Jung-shin's father works at the bank. Tae-yul hears of the Japanese attack on Pearl Harbor, Hawaii, and tells everyone. Uncle says he'll need Tae-yul to print special flyers for the Japanese. Tae-yul sees his first airplane. Neighborhood associations of ten households each are formed. At drills, the households count off. When an elderly neighbor woman is beaten because she can't speak her number in Japanese, Sun-hee teaches her to count to five in Japanese.

Vocabulary
dishonorable (38)
disobeyed (39)
doubtful (40)
intricate (42)
mesh (44)
garbled (46)
incredible (47)
regaining (56)

Discussion Questions

1. Tae-yul tiptoes to a window to eavesdrop on his uncle and father. Sun-hee tiptoes up to him so he can't tell her to go away or he'll be discovered. What does he think of this? What is the relationship between the brother and sister? *(He thinks it was a smart thing to do. Answers will vary. p. 38)*

2. Abuji believes that Koreans killing Koreans is worse than anything the Japanese can do to them. Why does he believe this? *(Koreans should be united, not destroying each other. He views the Japanese as the enemy. Answers will vary. p. 40)*

3. Uncle acts mysteriously when Sun-hee takes her friend to the print shop. Is she imagining his reaction? Why or why not? *(His reaction makes the reader think that he doesn't trust Jung-shin's father. Answers will vary. pp. 44–45)*

4. What type of movie is shown to teach the Korean students about Americans? Is this a fair representation of Americans? Why would the Japanese show a fiction movie instead of a nonfiction documentary about Americans? *(Onishi-san shows an old western movie of cowboys shooting black-haired Indians. The Japanese want the Korean people to hate and fear the Americans. Answers will vary. p. 50)*

5. Why does Mrs. Ahn refuse to learn the Japanese numbers for six through ten? What does this say about her character? *(She does not want to give her mind to the Japanese. She will only learn what is necessary so she will not be beaten. Answers will vary. p. 58)*

6. **Prediction:** Will Uncle get in trouble with the Japanese?

Supplementary Activities

1. Research: Find and make a recipe for *duk*, the sweetened rice cake.

2. Writing: Write a paragraph about a time you were mystified by someone's behavior and later learned why the person was acting in an odd fashion.

3. Foreshadowing: Recall that Uncle was beaten for putting the Olympic runner's Korean name in the newspaper. Now he's in danger again. Is it likely that he's involved in an activity against the Japanese? Write a paragraph explaining your viewpoint.

4. Metaphors and Similes: Add to your list of metaphors and similes: "words like ghosts hanging in the air" (p. 38).

5. History: Learn what day the Japanese bombed Pearl Harbor.

6. Language: Learn to count to ten in Japanese.

Chapters 12–15, pp. 59–81

As the war escalates, the Japanese take away the Koreans' radios, blankets, and warm clothes. Even Tae-yul's bicycle is commandeered. Tomo waits outside Sun-hee's home and talks to her about the little wire things her uncle made for them and how he hoped they were safe. She interprets this to mean Uncle is in danger, and she warns him. He goes into hiding. Later that night there is a neighborhood accounting. The soldiers want all metal items that aren't necessities. Sun-hee knows now that Tomo was warning her about the metal commandeering, not about her uncle. She cries herself to sleep.

Vocabulary
reign (59)
divine (60)
realm (63)
hastily (70)
spiel (75)
commandeering (75)
brooch (75)

Discussion Questions

1. How does Tae-yul feel about the rubber balls at first? What does this say about his character? Why does his attitude change? *(He thinks they are fun. He doesn't believe giving balls is a fair exchange for the rice, language, and names the Japanese have taken from them. Answers will vary. pp. 60–61)*

2. Why does Tae-yul think his father doesn't care that the Japanese have taken his bicycle? How is Tae-yul rude to his father? Do you think this is rude? Why or why not? *(Abuji doesn't resist when the soldiers take Tae-yul's bicycle. He questions his decision. Answers will vary. pp. 63–64)*

3. Is it understandable that Sun-hee misinterprets Tomo's hooded warning? Why or why not? What would you interpret from what you know about Uncle's strange behavior? *(She would have no way of knowing that the soldiers needed metal, so jumping to the conclusion that her uncle is in danger seems likely. Answers will vary. pp. 66–67)*

4. Why doesn't Uncle question Sun-hee's announcement that he's in danger? *(He has expected to be exposed, but has no idea when it might occur. p. 69)*

5. Tae-yul doesn't understand the complexities of the Japanese resistance. What does he mean by "...Uncle disobeying Abuji in order to be able to obey him one day" (p. 74)? *(Under Japanese control, the Korean way of life is being destroyed. Uncle wants to bring the old ways back, and then he can obey his brother.)*

6. Tae-yul disobeys his father by leaving the house, yet he doesn't realize he's disobeyed until he's already on his way to Uncle's shop. What does this say about his emotions at the time? *(Answers will vary. p. 76)*

7. Was Sun-hee's mistake made with a good heart? Justify your answer with examples from the book and what you know about her character. *(Her first concern was about Uncle, but she wanted to be the one to figure it out and to impart the news to Uncle and the others. Answers will vary. pp. 80–81)*

8. **Prediction:** Will Uncle be arrested?

Supplementary Activities

1. History: Research metal and paper drives in the United States during World War II and share the information with the class via oral reports.

2. Writing: Write a paragraph about the way Tae-yul interacts with his father compared to the way you interact with a parent or guardian.

3. Listing: Look at a picture of a bicycle and make a list of parts necessary to make a primitive bike like Tae-yul and his uncle made.

4. Writing: Write a paragraph about a mistake made with good intentions.

Chapters 16–18, pp. 81–105

The military police search the Kim home for signs of Uncle, now that they know he's missing. Abuji is taken to police headquarters for questioning. Tae-yul stays out of school to build a Japanese airstrip. Sun-hee rarely talks because she is so sad that she made Uncle leave when he did not have to. An American plane flies over the school and drops leaflets. Sun-hee hides one and takes it home. So does Tae-yul. Abuji reads the leaflet and burns both of them. He tells them the Americans know Korea is their friend and will not bomb the country. By 1944, there is no more schoolwork, but Sun-hee reports to school each day for preparations for enemy invasion. She starts a diary of events. Older girls are taken to work in factories. The military police search the Kim household in the middle of the night for treacherous writing. They burn Sun-hee's diary.

Vocabulary
illegal (81)
authorities (82)
contradict (85)
supervised (86)
allies (88)
edible (95)
endeavor (97)
treasonous (101)

Discussion Questions

1. When Abuji is taken to police headquarters for questioning, Omoni doesn't tell the children to go to bed, but lets them sit up with her late into the night. Why? *(She realizes that they cannot sleep until they know if their father is safe. p. 82)*

2. Why does Abuji allow Tae-yul to quit school to work on the airstrip? *(He knows that Tae-yul isn't learning the things he should at school. The topics they discuss in school are not scholarly endeavors; they are Japanese propaganda. Answers will vary. pp. 85–86)*

3. Sun-hee wonders if Korean thoughts can be written in Japanese (p. 93). Compare her idea of language thoughts with her elderly neighbor, Mrs. Ahn (p. 58). *(Mrs. Ahn thinks it's unpatriotic to express her Korean thoughts in a foreign language. Answers will vary.)*

4. Sun-hee is horrified that her friend Jung-shin's family could be *chin-il-pa*. Why does this upset her? *(She's upset because the* chin-il-pa *are as much the Koreans' enemy as the Japanese, and Uncle has been fighting their work. Answers will vary. pp. 98–100)*

5. How does Uncle's story of the Japanese cutting off his father's topknot reflect Tae-yul's understanding of his father? *(As a youth, Abuji did nothing to aid his father, and now Tae-yul has done nothing to aid his sister when her diary is burned. Tae-yul is older than his father was during the earlier incident. He now understands that the effort to resist is futile. Answers will vary. pp. 103–105)*

6. What is the tone of the book? Cite examples to support your answer. *(The tone is serious with national pride, loss of freedom, hardships of war, and both quiet and hostile political disobedience as elements of the novel. Answers will vary.)*

7. **Prediction:** Will the Americans bomb Korea?

Supplementary Activities

1. Science: Find the various uses for pine tar and pine roots.

2. History: Research General MacArthur and write a two-paragraph profile on his life.

3. Writing: Write a six-line poem, much like what Sun-hee wrote in her diary.

Chapters 19–23, pp. 105–126

Abuji tells Sun-hee that her diary was burned, but not her words. She vows to start a new diary. The family learns about *kamikazes* and knows the end of the war is near because Japan is so desperate. Sun-hee has missed her friendship with the girl whose father is a Japanese sympathizer. She renews the friendship, feeling that she and her friend are not responsible for their relatives' actions. Tae-yul is taken to police headquarters and told he needs to deliver a message to his uncle. Tae-yul will not betray his uncle and says he can't help the police because he has enlisted in the Japanese army. The Kim family takes the news hard, but Tae-yul tells Sun-hee the truth. After he's gone, she writes in her diary about it and feels like half of herself is gone.

Vocabulary
inflicted (107)
utmost (108)
accommodations (109)
reluctantly (112)
tactic (114)
recruits (114)
slander (117)
eliminate (118)
censored (122)
legibly (123)

Discussion Questions

1. Abuji tells Sun-hee that the words in her diary are not burned, only the paper. Sun-hee writes a poem about words and thoughts. How are words powerful? Explain your answer. *(Answers will vary. pp. 106–107)*

2. Sun-hee is afraid people will forget the idea of beauty. When people are trying just to survive, they have no time for observing blooming trees or nature greening or appreciating the color of the pearl in the dragon brooch. In your opinion, what is the correct place for art? *(Answers will vary. p. 110)*

3. Why does Sun-hee decide to renew her friendship with Jung-shin? *(She decides that the girl isn't responsible for what her father is doing, the same as she isn't responsible for what her uncle is doing. They are only children playing, and that's what they will continue to be. Answers will vary. pp. 111–112)*

4. Do you think Tae-yul's solution to protecting Uncle is too drastic? What else could he have done to avoid delivering a message to Uncle? *(Answers will vary. pp. 118–120)*

5. Why can't Sun-hee write the correct words about Tae-yul in her diary? What does this say about her relationship with her brother? *(She feels he took some of her thoughts with him. Answers will vary. p. 126)*

6. **Prediction:** Will Tae-yul be killed in the war?

Supplementary Activities

1. Research: Find out if there is a state art council in your state and what types of art it supports.

2. History: Research the role of kamikaze pilots in World War II. Is this tactic still in use today? (Refer to the suicide bombings in the Middle East.)

3. Writing: Write a few lines about an inanimate object in a code-like manner, much like Sun-hee did with the dragon brooch. Read your lines aloud and have others guess what object you are describing.

Chapters 24–27, pp. 126–149

Tae-yul reports for duty and is trained to be a soldier. Those who cannot live up to the commanding officers' orders experience brutal punishment. A Japanese soldier brings rice and fish to the Kim family. Sun-hee interprets Tae-yul's first letter to mean the war is going badly for the Japanese. Tae-yul overhears officers talk about how Koreans aren't brave enough to accept a special assignment, so he volunteers. He writes his family that he is being sent to Japan. Sun-hee interprets his letter to mean that he will be a suicide pilot. She asks Abuji to tell the authorities that he can't be trusted, even though that could mean he will be sent to a firing squad. Abuji tells the authorities, and they wait to see what the Japanese will do next.

Vocabulary
efficient (127)
obstacle (129)
recitation (130)
procedures (133)
tedious (135)
extraordinary (140)
survived (141)
revealed (146)

Discussion Questions

1. Tae-yul immediately sees the rose of Sharon blossom Sun-hee gave him as a dangerous item to possess. Later he realizes the man who's being beaten should not scream in pain or the beating will continue. What does this say about his intelligence? *(He is aware of what the Japanese will do; he reads them well. Answers will vary. pp. 127, 130)*

2. How does Omoni's attitude affect the way she receives the fish and rice? *(At first she thinks of them as being Japanese. Then she thinks that this is the good result that her son wanted for his sacrifice for the family. Answers will vary. p. 132)*

3. Is the Kim family *chin-il-pa* for having a son in the Japanese army and receiving Japanese food? *(Answers will vary.)*

4. Does Sun-hee correctly interpret Tae-yul's first letter? What does this say about her intelligence? *(Because the author gives both viewpoints, the reader can see that Sun-hee is correct in her assumptions. pp. 134–135)*

5. Tae-yul enjoys the family letters. What is "mother stuff"? *(His mother is worried about him, asks questions about his health, and gives unsolicited advice on how to stay well. Answers will vary. p. 138)*

6. Do you think Sun-hee has correctly interpreted the second letter? Will Abuji's explanation to the Japanese authorities make things better or worse? What would you do if you had this knowledge? *(Answers will vary. pp. 143, 149)*

7. **Prediction:** Will Tae-yul kill American soldiers?

Supplementary Activities

1. History: Find out what was put in a kit bag for United States soldiers during World War II.

2. Social Science: List qualities of a good soldier.

3. Writing: Pretend you are Tae-yul and write a letter home in such a way that Sun-hee can interpret a deeper meaning.

4. Research: Find and read "The Imperial Rescript to Soldiers and Sailors." The Internet would be a good source.

5. Science: Research when cherry trees blossom, so you can determine the time when Sun-hee and her family receive the second letter.

Chapters 28–29, pp. 149–170

It is only later that Tae-yul realizes he's volunteered to be a kamikaze. His excitement at learning to fly overshadows his fear of death. He doesn't want to help the Japanese by flying into an American ship, but he has a plan. He is thrilled about learning to fly and feels incredible freedom. He writes a final letter home before he is sent on his suicide mission. Sun-hee arrives home to hear her mother screaming. The family has received the box with Tae-yul's final letter. The family is in mourning. At a neighborhood accounting about two months later, the leader announces that Japan has surrendered. The war is over.

Vocabulary

casualties (154)
bombardment (154)
maneuvers (156)
evasive (156)
complicated (160)
spectacular (167)
grudgingly (168)

Discussion Questions

1. Why does Tae-yul believe he must fulfill his promise to be a kamikaze? Why do you think losing face is so important to him? *(He would lose face or honor completely if he backed down. Answers will vary. p. 150)*

2. Why does Tae-yul tell himself to expect that real flying will not be as good as he has imagined? Is this a good way to prepare yourself for unknown adventures? *(He doesn't want to be disappointed. Answers will vary. p. 155)*

3. How do the Kim family members react to receiving Tae-yul's box? Are these the reactions you would expect from these characters? *(Omoni screams and turns ashen; Abuji tries to speak and can't; Sun-hee's heart seems to stop beating, and her hands shake. Their grief is "too deep for tears." Answers will vary. pp. 164–166, 168)*

4. Explain Sun-hee's reaction to the news of the war's end. *(She is horrified that Tae-yul's death was less than two months earlier. She wants to howl at the futility of it. p. 170)*

Supplementary Activities

1. Metaphors and Similes: Add to your list of metaphors and similes. Example: "her body still as a stone" (p. 166).

2. History: Read about the surrender of the Japanese on the U.S.S. *Missouri*. Show pictures of the surrender with the Japanese in their dress attire.

3. Predictions: Complete the Prediction Chart on page 12 of this guide.

4. Science: Discover how a glider works and why it is effective in teaching flying lessons.

Chapters 30–32, pp. 170–192

The family learns about the dropping of the atomic bombs and the end of the war. They receive ration packages from the Americans. Sun-hee tells Tomo goodbye before he leaves for Japan. The family receives a packet that tells them that Uncle is in the northern part of Korea, but the Chinese are making it impossible for him to return home. Tae-yul comes home. Fog stopped his mission, and he was thrown in jail for failing to complete it. At the end of the war, he was released. He thinks his father is a coward until he learns that Abuji wrote for the resistance newspaper. Tae-yul plans to open Uncle's print shop. Sun-hee is learning the Korean alphabet and begins teaching Tae-yul.

Vocabulary
identity (174)
fidget (176)
apology (183)
filthy (184)
transplant (189)

Discussion Questions

1. Are you surprised at the way Sun-hee describes American soldiers? Why or why not? *(Answers will vary. p. 171)*

2. Along with food supplies, cigarettes are included in the ration package. Why would they be included? *(Studies had not yet been done to show the connection between smoking and cancer and heart disease. Answers will vary. p. 172)*

3. How does Sun-hee feel about Tomo? Why does she give him the stone? *(She is sorry he is going to a devastated country where he has never lived. He can take a part of Korea with him. p. 174)*

4. How do you think Tomo feels about leaving the only home he's ever known? Explain your answer. *(Answers will vary.)*

5. Does it surprise you that Mrs. Ahn has harbored resistance workers in her cellar? Why or why not? *(She showed great courage when she refused to learn the Japanese language or to count above five in Japanese, so it fits her character that she would work for the resistance. Answers will vary. p. 178)*

6. Why doesn't Tae-yul tell his family about the horrible conditions in prison? *(He does not want them to feel sorry for him. Answers will vary. p. 184)*

7. Why can't Tae-yul live with himself or a father he doesn't respect? *(The Korean culture demands respect of self and of parents. Answers will vary. p. 187)*

8. Sun-hee has forgiven herself for telling Uncle to flee. Do you feel she was wrong in telling him to hide earlier in the book? *(His activities could have been discovered at any time, so she has no way of knowing if she forced his premature hiding. Answers will vary. p. 190)*

9. **Prediction:** Will Uncle ever return to the Kim home?

Supplementary Activities

1. Science: Research the difference between types of rice grown in Southeast Asia and in the United States.

2. Plotting: Complete the Story Map on page 9 of this guide.

3. Research: Find a copy of the Korean alphabet. Learn to write your name in Korean.

4. Math: Find the total population of Korea and how many Japanese lived in Korea during World War II. Compute a percentage of Japanese compared to the entire population.

Post-reading Discussion Questions

1. Using three adjectives, describe Sun-hee as she was at the beginning of the novel and as she was at the end of the novel. Are your adjectives different? What do the different lists say about the changes in Sun-hee? Do the same exercise for Tae-yul. Which character do you feel you know better? *(Answers will vary.)*

2. Near the beginning of the book, Tae-yul knows more family secrets than Sun-hee, who is not supposed to hear the men talk. By the end of the book, Sun-hee has relayed family secrets about their father to Tae-yul. How has their relationship changed? *(Sun-hee has grown up. Tae-yul no longer sees Sun-hee as a pesky little sister but more as an equal.)*

3. From this novel, what have you learned about Korea during the Japanese occupation? *(Answers will vary.)*

4. How would things be different for Sun-hee and Tae-yul if their family had been *chin-il-pa*, a friend of the Japanese? *(Those who were friendly to the Japanese during the occupation are ostracized as enemies to the Korean people after the occupation ends.)*

5. What did you learn about the power of traditions from this book? *(Answers will vary.)*

6. What important lesson does Sun-hee learn about holding a person responsible for her family member's actions? *(Choices are ultimately made by individuals. Sun-hee can only make her own decisions. She cannot hold others responsible for consequences that result from her own choices, nor can she hold herself responsible for the choices others make.)*

7. How do you feel Uncle justified his involvement in the underground resistance, even though it could endanger his brother's family? *(Uncle felt the Korean nation was of more importance than a single family.)*

8. What do you think Sun-hee's life will be like in ten years? *(Answers will vary.)*

9. What did you learn about occupational government from this book? *(Answers will vary.)*

10. What do you think of kamikaze pilots? Can you draw a parallel to terrorists today? Explain your answer. *(Answers will vary but may include the concept that the pilot or terrorist is willing to sacrifice his or her own life to take the lives of others.)*

11. In the Author's Note, Linda Sue Park explains that she found a reference to the "empty cupboard" of Korean history between 1935 and 1945. She discovered the cupboard wasn't so empty. What did she find in it? *(Park found information through personal interviews, memoirs, and books written by others who had experienced the Japanese occupation.)*

12. Why is the novel called *When My Name Was Keoko*? *(The use of the name represents the period in the main character's life that is the focus of the story.)*

13. Would you change the part in the book where Tae-yul volunteers to become a kamikaze? Why or why not? *(Answers will vary.)*

14. Are there benefits as well as hardships to living in an occupied country? Explain your answer. *(Benefits could include: protection from other enemies, increased food supply, rebuilding of infrastructure. Hardships could include the loss of freedom, religious rights, jobs, culture, and individuality.)*

15. Do you feel Sun-hee and the other children at the school had their childhoods stolen as they learned to defend themselves against invasion? Why or why not? *(Answers will vary.)*

16. Would you write a letter or an article for an underground newspaper to express your opinion? Why or why not? *(Answers will vary.)*

17. Would you volunteer for military service? Why or why not? *(Answers will vary.)*

18. Would you recommend this book to a friend? Why or why not? *(Answers will vary.)*

Post-reading Extension Activities

1. Read a chapter from the book aloud with friends, each taking a different character's role.

2. Draw a floor plan of what you believe the Kim house looks like. Include the garden area.

3. Find a recipe for a Korean dish, prepare it, and serve it to the class.

4. Linda Sue Park has written about actual events that occurred in her parents' lives. Talk to your parents about their childhood experiences and make a list of potential story ideas.

5. Replot the story by making Uncle *chin-il-pa.*

6. Explain how the book would have changed if Tae-yul had taken a message to Uncle instead of enlisting in the army.

7. Read reviews of Linda Sue Park's *When My Name Was Keoko* on the Internet.

8. Read other books by Linda Sue Park (*Seesaw Girl, The Kite Fighters,* and *A Single Shard).*

9. Visit Linda Sue Park's Web site at www.lspark.com and e-mail her your thoughts on the book.

10. Pick one chapter in the book and draw an illustration that could go before the chapter number.

11. Make a time line of all the events in the book with short annotations and illustrations.

Assessment for *When My Name Was Keoko*

Assessment is an ongoing process. The following eleven items can be completed during the novel study. Once finished, the student and teacher will check the work. Points may be added to indicate the level of understanding.

Name _____ Date _____

Student	Teacher

1. Keep a literary journal as you read the book.

2. Write the rest of the story. What has happened to Uncle in northern Korea? Write a two-page ending for the story.

3. Give yourself credit for each vocabulary activity you complete.

4. Keep a character chart of those you meet in the book. Include name, appearance, and significance to plot.

5. Create collages of ideas and images significant to Sun-hee and Tae-yul.

6. Keep your writing about the book in a folder. Choose one of your best pieces to submit for evaluation.

7. Create a flow chart (see p. 13 of this guide) of the events in the book's plot.

8. Write a letter to the principal of your school giving your evaluation of this book for classroom use.

9. Discuss the Post-reading Discussion Questions with a partner. Write a multi-paragraph essay on one of them.

10. Choose one of the Post-reading Extension Activities to complete.

11. Write a two-page entry in Sun-hee's diary reflecting the depth of her despair after Uncle leaves because she misinterpreted Tomo's words.

Linking Novel Units® Lessons to National and State Reading Assessments

During the past several years, an increasing number of students have faced some form of state-mandated competency testing in reading. Many states now administer state-developed assessments to measure the skills and knowledge emphasized in their particular reading curriculum. The discussion questions and post-reading questions in this Novel Units® Teacher Guide make excellent open-ended comprehension questions and may be used throughout the daily lessons as practice activities. The rubric below provides important information for evaluating responses to open-ended comprehension questions. Teachers may also use scoring rubrics provided for their own state's competency test.

Please note: The Novel Units® Student Packet contains optional open-ended questions in a format similar to many national and state reading assessments.

Scoring Rubric for Open-Ended Items

3-Exemplary	Thorough, complete ideas/information Clear organization throughout Logical reasoning/conclusions Thorough understanding of reading task Accurate, complete response
2-Sufficient	Many relevant ideas/pieces of information Clear organization throughout most of response Minor problems in logical reasoning/conclusions General understanding of reading task Generally accurate and complete response
1-Partially Sufficient	Minimally relevant ideas/information Obvious gaps in organization Obvious problems in logical reasoning/conclusions Minimal understanding of reading task Inaccuracies/incomplete response
0-Insufficient	Irrelevant ideas/information No coherent organization Major problems in logical reasoning/conclusions Little or no understanding of reading task Generally inaccurate/incomplete response